All About
Me
My Family
Years Old
I Love....
Favorite Color
Favorite Food

ZOO
WELCOME
LET'S GO INSIDE

GROWL GROWL...

WHO SAYS GROWL?
GROWL GROWL..

MY NAME IS TIGER
I'M BIGGEST MEMBER OF CAT FAMILY
MY LITTLE ONES ARE CALLED CUBS
DONT COME NEAR OR I MIGHT BITE
I'M A FEARLESS KILLER OF DEER
TO HAVE MY DINNER
I LIVE IN DEN

BRR..BRR..

BRR..BRR..
WHO SAYS BRR..?

MY NAME IS GIRAFFE
I' AM THE TALLEST MAMMAL
I HAVE A LONG NECK THAT
HELPS ME FIND GOOD FOOD
MY LONG LEGS HELP ME GET
AWAY IF LIONS COME AROUND
I LIVE IN A GRASSLAND

HOO HOO HOO

HOO HOO HOO
WHO SAYS HOO HOO?

MY NAME IS MONKEY
I AM A NAUGHTY BOY
I LOVE EATING BANANAS
I ENJOY JUMPING FROM
TREE TO TREE
I STAY IN A TREE
WITH MY FAMILY

NEIGH..NEIGH

WHO SAYS NEIGH?
NEIGH..NEIGH

MY NAME IS ZEBRA
I LOOK LIKE A HORSE
I HAVE BLACK &WHITE STRIPES
ON MY BODY
I LOVE TO GRAZE ON
GRASS ALL DAY

ROAR......

ROAR......

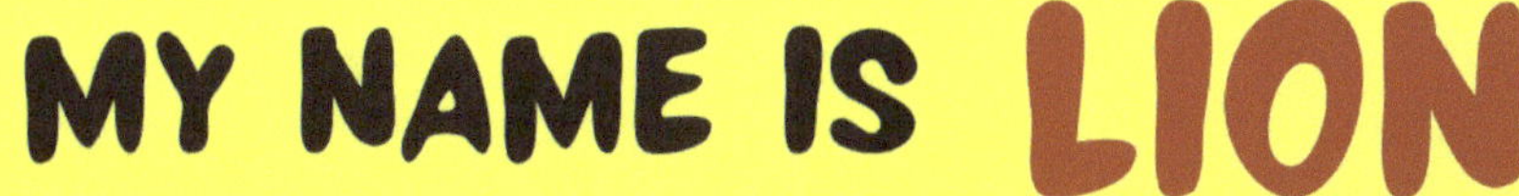

MY NAME IS LION

I AM THE KING OF THE FOREST

MY LITTLE ONES ARE CALLED CUB

I AM A CARNIVOROUS

THAT MEANS I EAT MEAT

I GO OUT FOR A HUNT

AT NIGHT TO HAVE MY

DINNER.

ART..ARF..ARF

WHO SAYS ARF?

MY NAME IS SEA LION
I LOVE ENTERTAINING PEOPLE'S
I CAN SWIM IN WATER
AND WALK IN LAND
I AM A CARNIVOROUS
AND I EAT
FISH,SQUID,CRABS,CLAMS

CLICK..CLICK

WHO SAYS CLICK?
CLICK..CLICK

MY NAME IS DOLPHIN
I AM KIDS FAVORITE
I CAN SWIM FAST AND
JUMP HIGH IN THE AIR
I CAN COMMUNICATE
WITH
WHISTLES,CLICKS,SQUEAKS
I EAT FISH

GROWL..GROWL

GROWL..GROWL
WHO SAYS GROWL?

MY NAME IS BEAR
I CLAIM TREES
TO SEARCH FOR HONEY
ISN'T IT FUNNY
I REST MYSELF IN DEN
I AM CARNIVOROUS

HISS..HISS

HISS..HISS
WHO SAYS HISS?

MY NAME IS **SNAKE**

I HAVE **POISON** IN MY TEETH

I AM A **CARNIVOROUS**

THAT MEANS MEAT EATER

I CRAWL ON THE GROUND AS I

DON'T HAVE LEGS

DON'T COME NEAR ME OR I

MIGHT **BITE**

NEEH..NEEH

NEEH..NEEH
WHO SAYS NEEH?

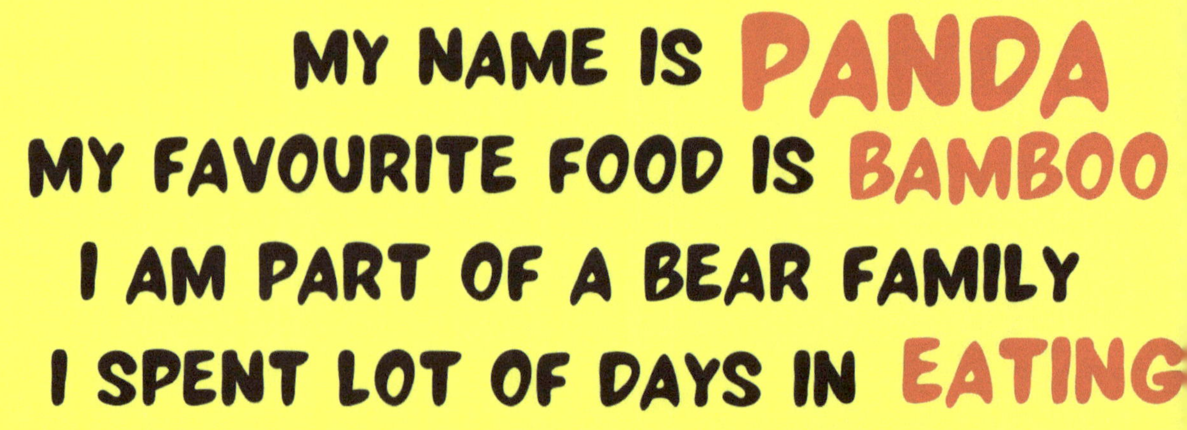

MY NAME IS PANDA
MY FAVOURITE FOOD IS BAMBOO
I AM PART OF A BEAR FAMILY
I SPENT LOT OF DAYS IN EATING
MY LITTLE ONES ARE
CALLED CUB
I CLAIM TREES TO
HAVE MY SNACK.

SQUAWK..SQUAWK

SQUAWK
WHO SAYS SQUAWK?

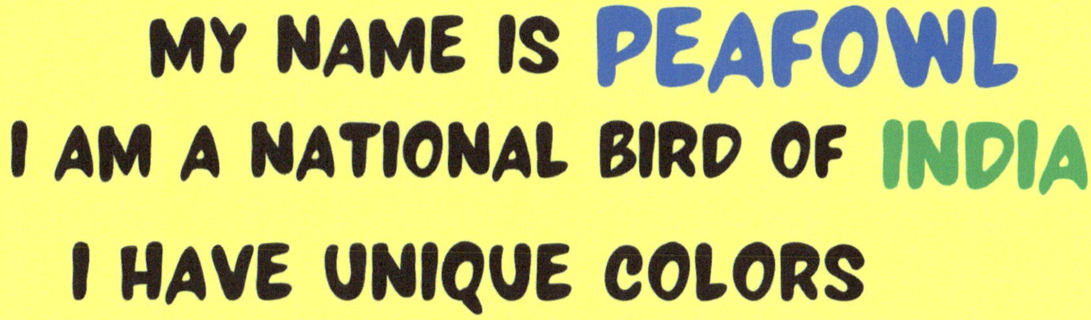

MY NAME IS PEAFOWL
I AM A NATIONAL BIRD OF INDIA
I HAVE UNIQUE COLORS
IN MY FEATHERS
I CAN FLY AND WALK
I EAT WORMS AND
STAY IN A TREE
MALE ONES ARE CALLED
PEACOCK
FEMALE ONES ARE CALLE
PEAHEN

GRUNT..GRUNT

WHO SAYS GRUNT?

MY NAME IS CROCODILE
I AM A REPTILE
I LIVE IN WATER
I HAVE SHARP TEETH
TO KILL MY PREY
I BITE STRONGER AND
I'M GOOD PREDACTOR

Noisy Zoo

THE BROWN BEAR GROWLS, WHEN
MONKEY CHATTERS IN THE TREE
HISS HISS GOES THE SNAKE.
LIONS ROAR AND THE TIGER ROAR
PEACOCK DANCE WHEN THE RAIN POURS
IN THE TREE, PANDA NEEH
WHEN THE DOLPHINS CLICK IN THE WATER

GOOD NIGHT
ZOO